God Made the Animals

Published by Standard Publishing, Cincinnati, Ohio
www.standardpub.com

Copyright © 1983, 2007 by Standard Publishing. All rights reserved. #45419. Manufactured in Cincinnati, OH, USA, June 2013. Happy Day logo and trade dress are trademarks of Standard Publishing. Printed in the United States of America. Illustrated by Nan Pollard. All Scripture quotations, unless otherwise indicated, are taken from the *International Children's Bible*®. Copyright © 1986, 1988, 1999, 2005 by Thomas Nelson, Inc. Used by permission. All rights reserved. Reproducible: Permission is granted to reproduce these pages for ministry purposes only—not for resale.

ISBN-13: 978-0-7847-2005-9
ISBN-10: 0-7847-2005-3

18 17 16 15 14 13   5 6 7 8 9 10 11 12 13

Cincinnati, Ohio

God made the deer.
"Let the earth be filled with animals." *Genesis 1:24*

God made the turtle.

God made the squirrel.

God made the rabbit.

"God . . . created every living thing that moves in the sea." *Genesis 1:21*

God made the kitten.

God made the dog.

God made the donkey.

God made the chicken.

God made the cow.

God made the pig.

God made the goat.

God made the horse.

God made the lamb.

"God . . . made every bird that flies." *Genesis 1:21*